THE OFFICIAL

BIONICLE

by Greg Farshtey

Puffin

To the LEGO Company, for creating an amazing universe and letting me play in it – G. F.

PUFFIN BOOKS

Published by the Penguin Group
Penguin Books Ltd, 80 Strand, London WC2R 0RL, England
Penguin Putnam Inc., 375 Hudson Street, New York, New York 10014, USA
Penguin Books Australia Ltd, 250 Camberwell Road, Camberwell, Victoria 3124, Australia
Penguin Books Canada Ltd, 10 Alcorn Avenue, Toronto, Ontario, Canada M4V 3B2
Penguin Books India (P) Ltd, 11 Community Centre, Panchsheel Park, New Delhi – 110 017, India
Penguin Books (NZ) Ltd, Cnr Rosedale and Airborne Roads, Albany, Auckland, New Zealand
Penguin Books (South Africa) (Pty) Ltd, 24 Sturdee Avenue, Rosebank 2196, South Africa

Penguin Books Ltd, Registered Offices: 80 Strand, London WC2R 0RL, England

www.penguin.com

First published in the USA by Scholastic Inc. 2003
Published in Great Britain in Puffin Books 2003
1 3 5 7 9 10 8 6 4 2

Copyright © The LEGO Group, 2003
LEGO, the LEGO logo, BIONICLE™, and the BIONICLE™ logo are registered trademarks of
The LEGO Group and are used here by special permission
All rights reserved

Set in GillSans 12 on 16pt

Made and printed in Italy by Printer Trento Srl

Except in the United States of America, this book is sold subject to the condition that it shall not, by way of trade or otherwise, be lent, re-sold, hired out, or otherwise circulated without the publisher's prior consent in any form of binding or cover other than that in which it is published and without a similar condition including this condition being imposed on the subsequent purchaser

British Library Cataloguing in Publication Data
A CIP catalogue record for this book is available from the British Library

ISBN 0–141–31735–3

LIVE THE LEGEND

This *Official Guide to BIONICLE*™ is your introduction to a universe full of action and excitement! These cool LEGO characters have an even cooler story behind them. If you've ever been to **www.bionicle.com** you may even know some of it already. But here, for the **first time ever**, you'll find the entire BIONICLE™ legend. This is your complete guide to the BIONICLE™ universe, with everything there is to know about its awesome adventures!

IN THE TIME
BEFORE TIME . . .

In the time before time, a great being called **Mata Nui** brought his people, the **Matoran,** to an island paradise. The Matoran lived happily under his loving protection. They even named the island Mata Nui, in his honour.

But a shadow soon fell over the land. Mata Nui had a powerful brother, **Makuta**. Makuta was jealous of Mata Nui and all he created. He cast a spell that made his brother, Mata Nui, fall into a deep sleep. Then Makuta took power over the land. Fields withered away, sunlight grew cold and the ancient values of the Matoran were gradually forgotten.

Still, all hope was not lost. Legends spoke of six mighty heroes, called the **Toa**. According to the legend, the Toa would arrive to rescue the island and its people from the darkness. The Matoran waited a long, long time for these heroes to arrive – and one day, they finally did.

Six Toa washed ashore: Tahu, Kopaka, Gali, Lewa, Pohatu and Onua. The Toa did not know who they were or where they had come from, but they knew they shared a great destiny: to defeat Makuta and save Mata Nui.

Mata Nui gave the Matoran three values to live by: **unity, duty** and **destiny**. For many years, the Matoran held these values above all else. But when the shadow of Makuta fell over the land, the Matoran began to forget about the old ways. Perhaps the Toa, through their brave deeds, will bring unity, duty and destiny back to the land.

MATA NUI

- Po-Koro
- Abandoned caves
- Onu-Koro
- Ga-Koro
- Ko-Koro
- Kini-Nui
- Ta-Koro
- Makuta's underground lair
- Mangai lava falls
- Le-Koro

THE MATORAN ALPHABET

The people of Mata Nui have their own language. Use this page to decode the secret Matoran messages you'll find in this book!

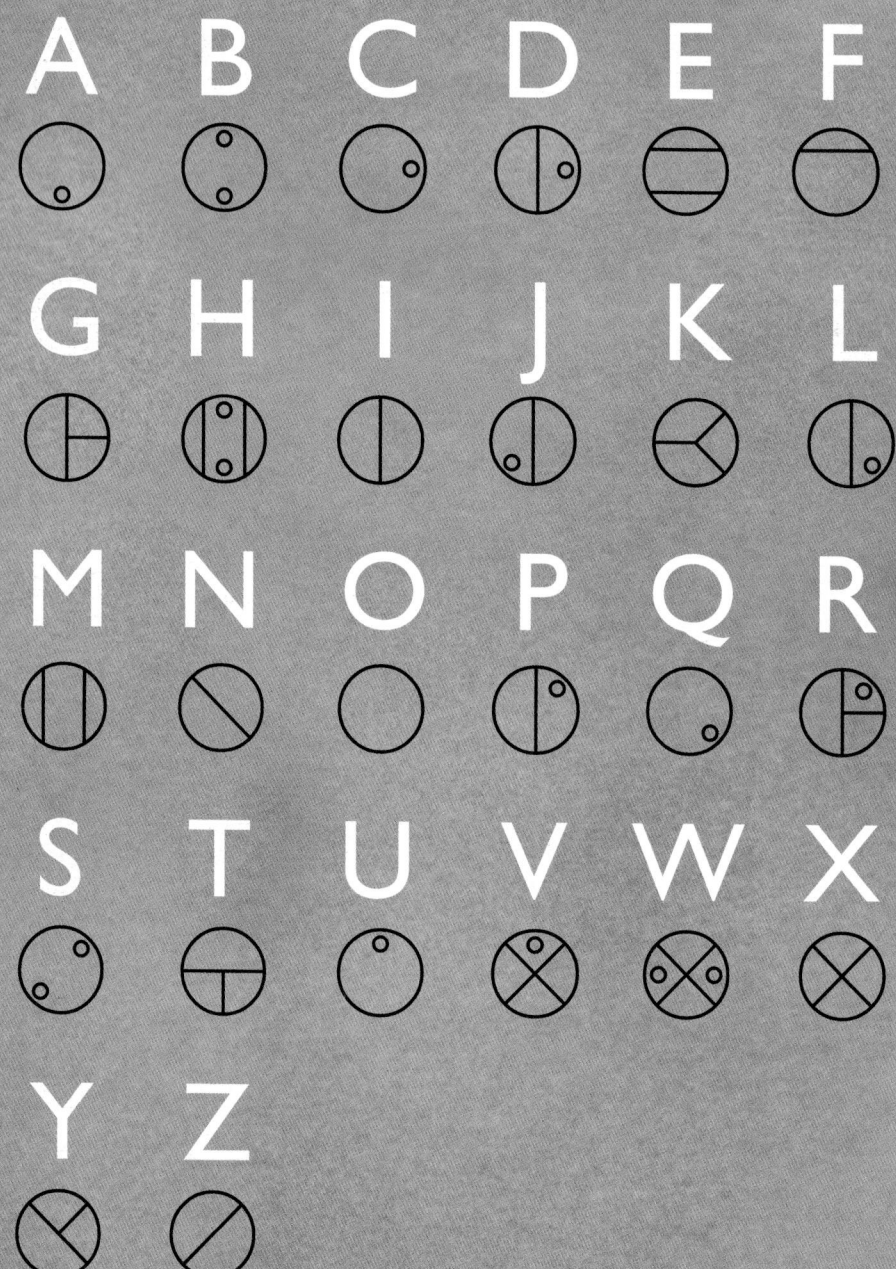

HEROES AND VILLAINS

The island of Mata Nui is home to many different kinds of BIONICLE™ characters. Some are good, some are evil – and you will meet them all in this book, including:

- **Toa** (TOE-ah): Six mighty heroes who protect the island; now known as **Toa Nuva**
- **Turaga** (too-RAH-gah): Village elders
- **Matoran** (mat-OR-ran): Brave and hardworking villagers
- **Makuta** (mah-KOO-tah): Master of shadows; the Toa's worst enemy
- **Rahi** (RAH-hee): Powerful beasts who serve Makuta
- **Bohrok** (BOE-rok): Insect-like beings who threaten Mata Nui in swarms
- **Bohrok-Kal** (BOE-rok KAHL): A special squad of ultrapowerful Bohrok
- **Rahkshi** (RAHK-shee): Six dangerous hunters who do Makuta's will

Matoran Message:

TOA NUVA

In Mata Nui's darkest hour, six heroes called the **Toa** arrived to defend the island and its people. After many difficult battles and great triumphs, they gained new armour, new tools, new powers and a new name. The Toa are now known as the **Toa Nuva**. But their mission remains the same: to defeat Makuta and save the island.

Tahu Nuva

Pronunciation: TAH-hoo NOO-vah

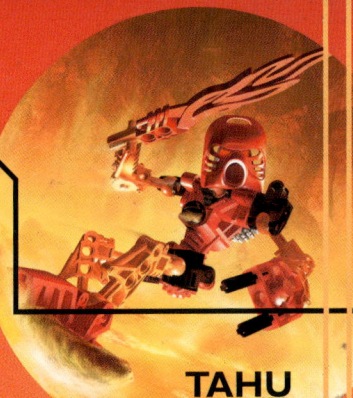
TAHU

Colour: Red
Element: Fire
Village: Ta-Koro
Powers:
- Can create fire
- Can melt any substance
- Can withstand extreme heat

Tools: Two magma swords that channel his power; can be joined together to form a lava board, for surfing on molten magma

Mask: Kanohi Hau Nuva, the Great Mask of Shielding

Tahu Nuva's bravery and strength have made him the leader of the Toa. His temper is as legendary as his powers, but he tries hard to keep it in check. He is fearless and will challenge any foe to protect his village and his people.

TAHU NUVA

ONUA

Onua Nuva

Pronunciation: oh-NOO-ah NOO-vah

Colour: Black
Element: Earth
Village: Onu-Koro
Powers:
- Can tunnel through any substance
- Can cause earthquakes
- Night vision

Tools: Two quake-breakers that can tunnel through earth and rock; can be attached to his feet and used as all-terrain treads
Mask: Kanohi Pakari Nuva, the Great Mask of Strength

Onua Nuva is the wisest of the Toa. He speaks only when he has something important to say and is always willing to help his friends. He is trusted and respected by all.

ONUA NUVA

Gali Nuva

Pronunciation: GAH-lee NOO-vah

GALI

Colour: Blue
Element: Water
Village: Ga-Koro
Powers:
- Commands water – can create tidal waves, whirlpools and floods
- Can swim faster than any known underwater creature
- Can sense changes in the natural world

Tools: Two aqua axes, powerful enough to slice through the toughest undersea obstacles; can also be used as scuba fins for faster speeds underwater

Mask: Kanohi Kaukau Nuva, the Great Mask of Water Breathing

Gali Nuva is the only female Toa. She is gentle, kind, and peaceful – but if the people of Ga-Koro are threatened, she will not hesitate to use all of her awesome powers in their defence.

GALI NUVA

Kanohi Masks of Power

Many of the BIONICLE™ characters get their great powers from the masks they wear. There are many different kinds of masks, including **Great Masks**, **Golden Kanohi Masks** and **Kanohi Nuva Masks**. Each type of mask supplies a different power and each kind of BIONICLE™ wears a different type.

- There are 36 Great Masks in total – six different masks for each of the six Toa.

- When the Toa had gathered all of the Great Masks of Power, they were each rewarded with a Gold Mask. Each Gold Mask has the power of all six types of Great Mask.

- When the Toa were transformed into the Toa Nuva, they had to collect a new set of masks: the Kanohi Nuva.

Great Masks of Power

There are six types of Great Masks. When the Toa first arrived on the island of Mata Nui, each of them had one Great Mask. But they were not powerful enough to take on Makuta. So the Toa went on a dangerous quest to collect all the Great Masks.

Matoran Message:

Kanohi Akaku
The Great Mask of X-Ray Vision
Allows the user to see through walls and discover that which is hidden.
Worn by Kopaka when he first washed ashore.

Kanohi Hau
The Great Mask of Shielding
Protects the user against attacks but has no effect against ambushes.
Worn by Tahu when he first washed ashore.

Kanohi Kakama
The Great Mask of Speed
Allows the user to move great distances in an instant.
Worn by Pohatu when he first washed ashore.

Kanohi Kaukau
The Great Mask of Water Breathing
Allows the user to breathe underwater.
Worn by Gali when she first washed ashore.

Kanohi Miru
The Great Mask of Levitation
Allows the user to glide on air currents and descend from great heights safely.
Worn by Lewa when he first washed ashore.

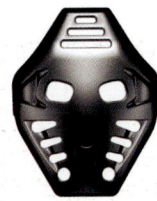

Kanohi Pakari
The Great Mask of Strength
Increases the user's physical power.
Worn by Onua when he first washed ashore.

LEWA

Lewa Nuva

Pronunciation: lay-WAH NOO-vah

Colour: Green
Element: Air
Village: Le-Koro

Powers:
- Can control wind, creating tornadoes and hurricanes
- Commands the air – can calm windstorms
- Can combine his power with Gali Nuva to create thunderstorms

Tools: Two sharp blades that can cut through dense jungle growth; can also be used as glider wings, allowing him to soar above the trees

Mask: Kanohi Miru Nuva, the Great Mask of Levitation

LEWA NUVA is rash, bold, and often plunges into situations without considering the danger. His experiences have given him respect for the perils of Mata Nui. But he still loves adventure and exploration.

LEWA NUVA

Protodermis

Very little is known about the strange substance known as protodermis. The Matoran of Onu-Koro have been mining it for many years as a source of energy, but even they are uncertain of what it is or where it comes from.

After a huge underground battle, the Toa fell into large tubes filled with protodermis. They returned to the surface with new armour, new tools and new powers. The Toa are now more powerful than ever. This is why they have given themselves a new name: Toa Nuva.

KOPAKA

Kopaka Nuva

Pronunciation: koh-PAH-kah NOO-vah

Colour: Silver
Element: Ice
Village: Ko-Koro

Powers:
- Can create storms of snow or ice
- Can freeze any substance
- Can withstand extreme cold

Tool: Ice blade that channels his power; can be split in two and used as power ice-skates

Mask: Kanohi Akaku Nuva, the Great Mask of X-Ray Vision

Kopaka Nuva does not like being part of a team. He is very clever and likes to deal with problems on his own. The other Toa Nuva think he is unfriendly, but they also respect his intelligence and his instincts.

KOPAKA NUVA

Kanohi Nuva

The **Kanohi Nuva** masks are the most powerful of all Masks of Power.

There are a total of 36 Kanohi Nuva masks – six different masks for each of the six Toa Nuva. A Kanohi Nuva allows the user to share its energies with those nearby.

Kanohi Akaku Nuva, *The Great Mask of X-Ray Vision*
Allows the user to see through walls and illusions.

Kanohi Hau Nuva, *The Great Mask of Shielding*
Protects against the most powerful attacks, but not against ambushes.

Kanohi Kakama Nuva, *The Great Mask of Speed*
Allows the user to move at great speed and pass through solid objects without harm.

Kanohi Kaukau Nuva, *The Great Mask of Water Breathing*
Allows the user to breathe underwater.

Kanohi Miru Nuva, *The Great Mask of Levitation*
Allows the user to soar into the air and reach amazing heights.

Kanohi Pakari Nuva, *The Great Mask of Strength*
Increases the strength of the user.

POHATU

Pohatu Nuva

Pronunciation: poe-HAH-too NOO-vah

Colour: Brown
Element: Stone
Village: Po-Koro

Powers:
- Enormous strength
- Can smash rocks with his fists
- Can throw giant boulders at his enemies

Tools: Two climbing claws, which help him scale the rocky peaks near his home; can be combined to form a ball

Mask: Kanohi Kakama Nuva, the Great Mask of Speed

Pohatu Nuva is loyal, noble and trustworthy, and considers all the other Toa Nuva to be his friends. He is the strongest of all the Toa and can be relied upon in any situation.

POHATU NUVA

The Toa of Light

Only six Toa have washed ashore on Mata Nui – but according to legend, there is a seventh Toa. Legend says that he will appear to the Matoran and lead them against Makuta, freeing the island from shadows for all time.

How much of this legend is true? No one knows for sure. Only time will tell whether the story is fact or fiction. Listed below is all that is known about this mysterious seventh Toa.

Element: Light
Colour: Unknown
Village: Unknown
Powers:
- Can turn darkness into day
- Can change the anger of an enemy into friendship

Tools: Matoran carvings show the Toa of Light carrying a staff of some sort, but its use is unknown. The myths also describe him as having a great vehicle, capable of tunnelling below the surface at amazing speeds. This vehicle will lead him directly to Makuta.
Mask: Kanohi Avohkii, the Great Mask of Light

A Kanohi mask resembling the legendary Mask of Light has been found by two Matoran, Takua and Jaller of Ta-Koro. They are, at present, on a journey to find the seventh Toa.

TURAGA

Each of the six villages on Mata Nui is ruled by an elder called a **Turaga**. As the oldest and wisest member of the village, the Turaga's job is to be sure the ancient legends are not forgotten. The Turaga work together to protect the knowledge of Mata Nui's past, as well as the prophecies about its future.

Turaga Vakama

Pronunciation: too-RAH-gah vah-KAH-mah

Colour: Red

Village: Ta-Koro

Mask: Kanohi Huna, the Noble Mask of Concealment

Tool: Fire staff

Turaga Vakama is known for his great courage and his hot temper.

Noble Masks of Power

Noble Masks of Power can be worn by either Toa or Turaga; they are most often used by Turaga. They have less energy than the Great Masks. There are a total of 36 Noble Masks – the Toa collected all 36 and returned them to their villages.

Kanohi Huna, *The Noble Mask of Concealment*
Allows the wearer to become invisible.
Worn by Turaga Vakama of Ta-Koro.

Kanohi Komau, *The Noble Mask of Mind Control*
Allows the wearer to make others do his bidding.
Worn by Turaga Onewa of Po-Koro.

Kanohi Mahiki, *The Noble Mask of Illusion*
Allows the wearer to deceive an enemy by creating illusions.
Worn by Turaga Matau of Le-Koro.

Kanohi Matatu, *The Noble Mask of Telekinesis*
Allows the wearer to move objects using the power of his thoughts.
Worn by Turaga Nuju of Ko-Koro.

Kanohi Rau, *The Noble Mask of Translation*
Allows the wearer to read ancient languages, runes and symbols.
Worn by Turaga Nokama of Ga-Koro.

Kanohi Ruru, *The Noble Mask of Night Vision*
Allows the wearer to see in total darkness.
Worn by Turaga Whenua of Onu-Koro.

Turaga Whenua

Pronunciation: too-RAH-gah wen-NOO-ah

Colour: Black

Village: Onu-Koro

Mask: Kanohi Ruru, the Noble Mask of Night Vision

Tool: Drill of Onua

Turaga Whenua is known for his honesty. As he often says, 'It serves no purpose to be false, for the earth cannot be deceived.'

Turaga Nokama

Pronunciation: too-RAH-gah noh-KAH-mah

Colour: Blue

Village: Ga-Koro

Mask: Kanohi Rau, the Noble Mask of Translation

Tool: Trident

Turaga Nokama is the only female Turaga. She is famous for her ability to resolve disputes among the other village elders.

Turaga Matau

Pronunciation: too-RAH-gah mah-TOW

Colour: Green

Village: Le-Koro

Mask: Kanohi Mahiki, the Noble Mask of Illusion

Tool: Kau Kau staff

Turaga Matau is always calm in a crisis. He is famous all over the island for his sense of humour.

Turaga Nuju

Pronunciation: too-RAH-gah NOO-joo

Colour: Silver

Village: Ko-Koro

Mask: Kanohi Matatu, the Noble Mask of Telekinesis

Tool: Great ice pick

Turaga Nuju is an excellent storyteller, although he never speaks. Nuju communicates only through whistles and gestures. A Matoran named Matoro stays by his side to interpret.

Turaga Onewa

Pronunciation: too-RAH-gah oh-NEE-wah

Colour: Brown

Village: Po-Koro

Mask: Kanohi Komau, the Noble Mask of Mind Control

Tool: Great stone hammer

Turaga Onewa is nicknamed the Referee for his swift decisions and willingness to stand behind them.

THE SECRETS OF THE TURAGA

Since the Toa arrived on Mata Nui, the Turaga have been there to provide them with important information. The Toa learned about the Kanohi masks and the Bohrok swarms from the Turaga, and they have come to rely on the wisdom of the village elders.

But often it seems that the Turaga know more than they are telling. There are caverns that they have forbidden any Matoran to enter, but they will not say why. Some Toa Nuva have questioned why they were not told about the Bohrok before the swarms appeared on the island. It may be that the Turaga keep many more secrets than anyone knows . . .

Matoran Message:

MATORAN

The Matoran of Mata Nui live in six villages, called **koro**. The villages are spread out in different regions of Mata Nui. They all are distinct and have very different kinds of buildings, as well as customs. Although the Matoran are very loyal to their native villages, *all* Matoran share a common dream: to defeat Makuta and live in a land of peace and beauty.

Ta-Koro

 *Toa:* Tahu Nuva

 *Turaga:* Vakama

Villagers: Ta-Matoran

The village of Ta-Koro rises from the Lake of Fire near the mighty Mangai volcano. Its people live within dwellings made of cooled lava and work the lava fields to the north. A small lava stream flows through the village, providing it with heat. When they are not at work, the Ta-Matoran surf the lava rapids.

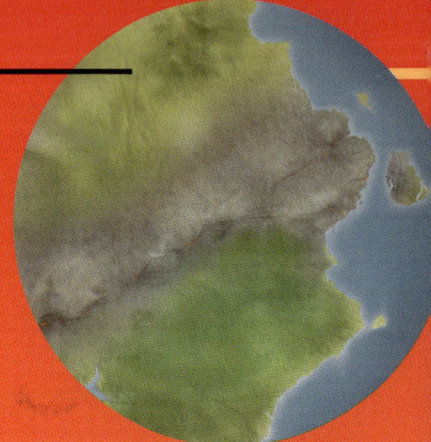

Jaller

Pronunciation: JAH-luh

Colour: Yellow

- Captain of the Ta-Koro Guard
- Responsible and dedicated to his job
- Best friends with Takua the Chronicler

Onu-Koro

 **Toa:** Onua Nuva

 **Turaga:** Whenua

Villagers: Onu-Matoran

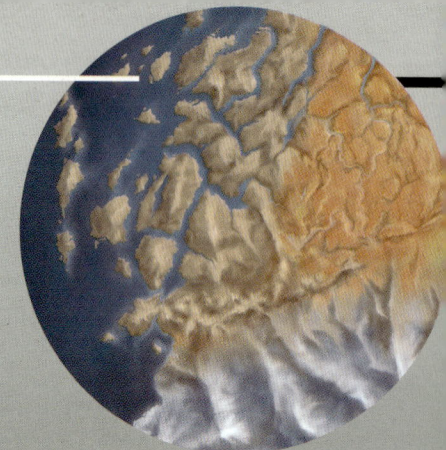

Onu-Koro is a village of dark tunnels, caves and mines that plunge deep beneath the surface of the island. The Onu-Matoran mine protodermis, compete in Ussal crab races, and listen closely for the vibrations that warn of danger approaching. When the Matoran are in danger, Onu-Koro is a good place to hide. In the worst of times, Onu-Koro tunnels have been used to get messages from one village to another. Onu-Matoran can see in the dark and their eyes are sensitive to bright light.

Onepu

Pronunciation: oh-NEE-poo

Colour: Purple

- Captain of the Ussalry, the Onu-Koro defence force
- Champion of the Great Ussal Crab Race for the last five seasons in a row

Nuparu

Pronunciation: new-PAH-roo

Colour: Orange

- Invented the **Boxor**, a vehicle used against the Bohrok swarms
- Always observing, learning and planning new inventions

Matoran Message:

Ga-Koro

Toa: Gali Nuva

Turaga: Nokama

Villagers: Ga-Matoran

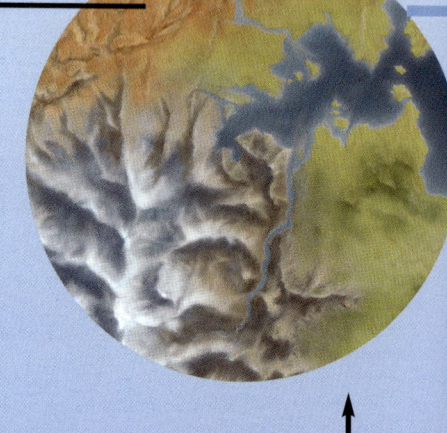

Climb the white cliffs above Gali's bay and far below you will see the village of Ga-Koro, floating in the waters off the north-eastern tip of Mata Nui. Built of seaweed, Ga-Koro is home to the brave Ga-Matoran. All of the Ga-Matoran are female, like their protector, Gali. Although Takua of Ta-Koro has visited in the past, Ga-Koro sees few travellers. The whirlpools and strong currents that surround the village are enough to keep most others away.

Macku

Pronunciation: MAH-koo

Colour: Blue

- Patrols the coast of Lake Naho from Ta-Wahi to Po-Wahi
- A talented all-round athlete who enjoys competing against Hewkii, her friend from Po-Koro

Le-Koro

   ***Toa:*** Lewa Nuva

   ***Turaga:*** Matau

             Villagers: Le-Matoran

Although the treetop village of Le-Koro is disguised to look like hanging jungle weeds, this was not enough to fool the Bohrok. The village was heavily damaged by the Lehvak and has only recently been rebuilt. Now the tall trees are once again alive with the chatter of Le-Matoran...but the swamp below remains a fearful place where none dare go.

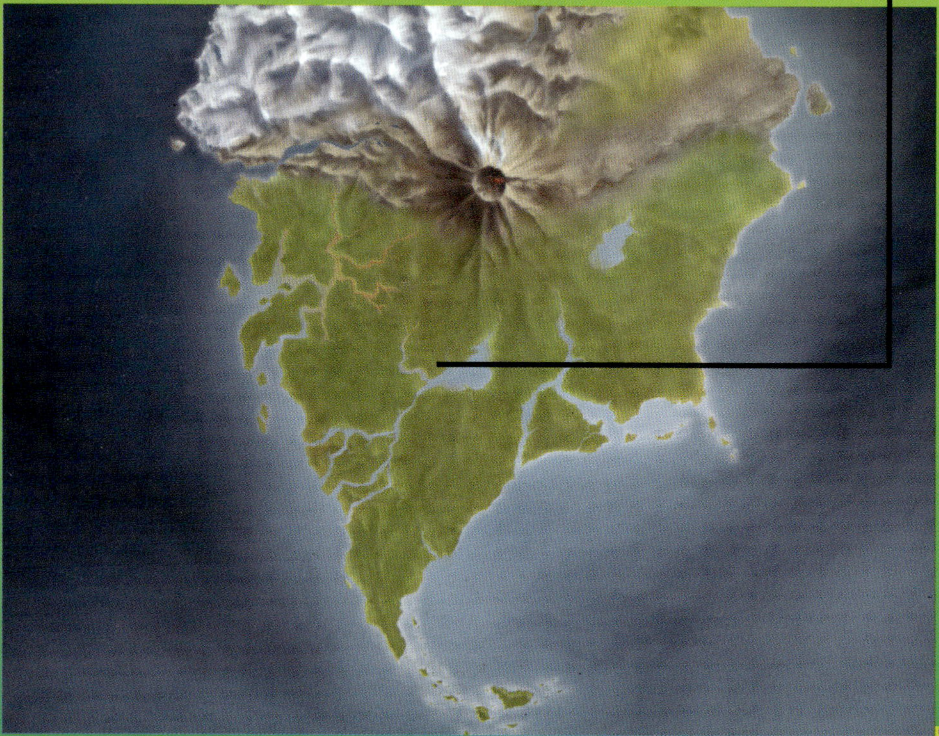

Kongu

Pronunciation: KON-goo

Colour: Green

- Captain of the Le-Koro Gukko Bird Force, which defends the village against all dangers
- An expert bird wrangler, pilot and navigator

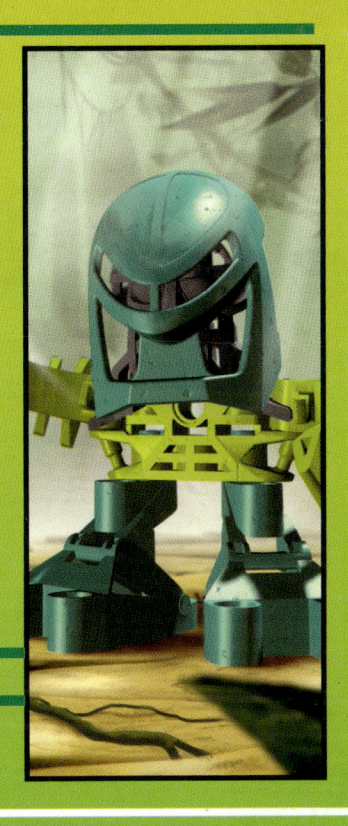

Le-Koro Slang

The Le-Matoran are the only Matoran with a special language of their own. It acts like a code to keep their enemies from knowing what they are talking about. Of course, their friends get pretty confused, too!

Cloudsneaking: Under cover of the clouds
Darktime: Dangerous or sad times
Deepwood: Deep in the jungle
Downtree: Lower in the tree
Everquick: Very fast
High-flying: Airborne
Highjump: Leap
Highlifting: Elevating
Leafdawn: Springtime
Lifedawn: Youth
Lowduck: Crouch
Quickdodge: Difficult to strike
Sunsoaring: Flying high above the treetops
Topleaf: As high as the treetops
Treebound: Unable to fly
Uptree: Higher in the tree
Wayfinder: Navigator

Ko-Koro

Toa: Kopaka Nuva

Turaga: Nuju

Villagers: Ko-Matoran

The ice village of Ko-Koro is hidden beneath a huge ice block that separates two glaciers. Enormous crevasses dot the surrounding mountains, into which a traveller can disappear forever. Master trackers and trap-builders, the Ko-Matoran have aided many other villages in the struggle against the Rahi and the Bohrok.

Matoro

Pronunciation: mat-OR-oh

Colour: Bluish silver

- Acts as interpreter for Turaga Nuju, translating his gestures and whistles into words
- Has seen much of the island, as he travels everywhere Nuju goes

Po-Koro

Toa: Pohatu Nuva

Turaga: Onewa

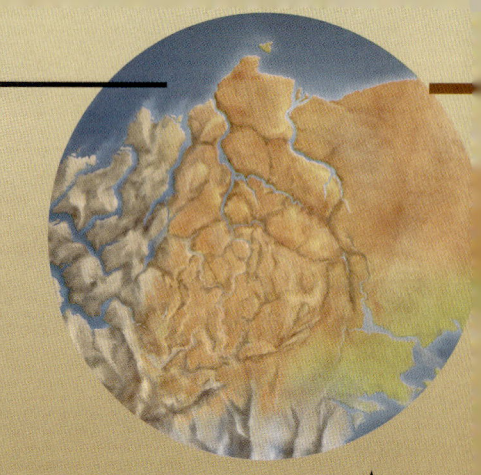

Villagers: Po-Matoran

The village of Po-Koro is located in the desert of the far north. All the structures in Po-Koro are built from rock and sand, and are designed to blend in with the surrounding area. Here the Po-Matoran carve stone into intricate forms, which they then trade to other villages for goods they need. The Po-Matoran love living in their barren, rocky wastelands because they hate water and cannot swim.

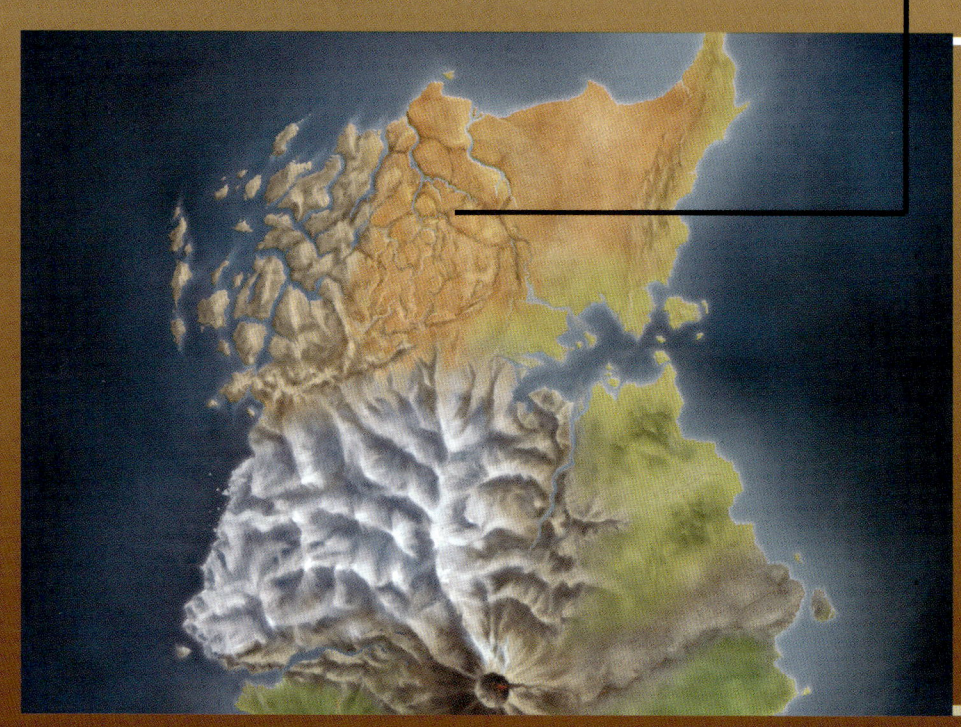

Hewkii

Pronunciation: HOO-kee

Colour: Brown

- The all-time top scorer at the sport of kolhii
- One of the few Matoran strong enough to crush boulders with his head as well as his feet

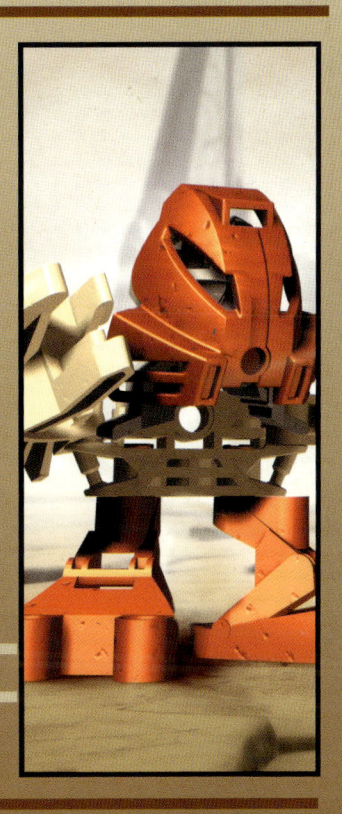

Kolhii

Although the Matoran love many sports, **kolhii** is by far the most popular. It is played all over Mata Nui.

Kolhii is played between two and six teams at a time, using kolhii balls (lightweight airstone bound in steel) and kolhii staffs (a long staff with a mallet-like hammer on one end and a scooped hurler at the other).

Players score goals by getting the kolhii ball into an opponent's net. The first team to reach the agreed-upon number of goals (usually three to five) wins.

MAKUTA

For many, many generations, the evil **Makuta** has ruled the island of Mata Nui. He is the subject of more myths and legends than any other being on the island. But little is truly known about him. He dwells far below the surface in a shadowy lair that no Matoran has ever entered.

No one has ever seen Makuta and returned to tell of it – even the Toa saw only one small part of his true form.

It is Makuta's will that Mata Nui remain asleep forever. To accomplish this, he will reduce the island to rubble, send countless menaces against the Matoran villages and challenge the Toa Nuva to try to stop him. Makuta will try to tempt Toa Nuva and Matoran into betraying their friends. He wears **Kanohi Kraahkan**, the Mask of Shadows, which can be used to turn friends against each other or fill the heart of the bravest hero with fear.

Legends say that only the Toa of Light will have the courage to resist Makuta's dark powers and end his reign forever.

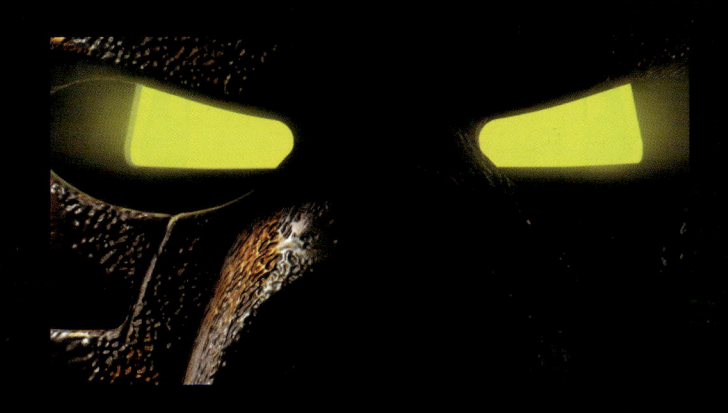

Matoran Message:

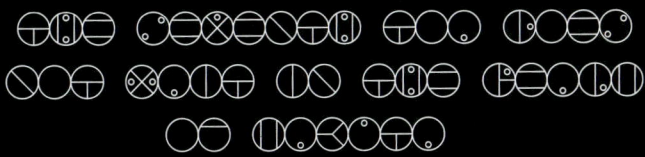

RAHI

The **Rahi** are the beasts of Mata Nui. In their natural state, they pose little threat to the Matoran. But when Makuta fitted the most powerful Rahi with infected **Masks of Power**, the Rahi became servants to Makuta's dark will. Makuta used them to guard the hiding places of the powerful Kanohi masks, which the Toa desperately needed.

The Toa eventually defeated most of Makuta's Rahi, removing their infected masks and taming them. Those Rahi that were not captured still lurk in the more remote regions of Mata Nui.

Tarakava

Pronunciation: TAH-rah-kah-vah

Region: Ga-Wahi
- Lizard-like creatures that live in coastal waters
- Prefer to ambush opponents and use their incredibly strong forelegs to strike

Nui-Rama

Pronunciation: Noo-ee RAH-mah

Region: Le-Wahi
- Insect-like creatures capable of flight; powerful enough to lift a Toa high into the air
- In battle, they use speed, stealth and stinger

Muaka & Kane-Ra

Pronunciation: moo-AH-kah & kah-NAY-rah

Region: Ko-Wahi
- Muaka resembles a huge tiger with sharp teeth and claws
- Kane-Ra looks like a massive bull

Nui-Jaga

Pronunciation: NOO-ee JAH-guh

Region: Po-Wahi
- Scorpion-like creatures that use their stingers to knock masks off their opponents
- Slow and not very bright

Matoran Message:

Manas

Pronunciation: MAH-nuhz

Most species of Rahi are not very smart. They use their strength – not their wits – to battle their opponents.

But the most dangerous Rahi, the **Manas**, were both smart and strong. These gigantic, crab-like creatures served as guards of Makuta's underground lair. No single Toa could hope to overcome the Manas. Only by merging their forms into the two Toa Kaita, were the heroes of Mata Nui able to defeat these creatures.

No Manas have been seen on the island for more than a year. But that does not mean they have gone . . . There could be others hiding deep beneath the surface, just waiting for Makuta's call.

BOHROK

When the Toa defeated the Rahi, Makuta unleashed a new menace: the **Bohrok**. Swarms of these insect-like creatures swept over the island, bringing chaos wherever they went. Like the Toa, they drew their powers from the elements. But the Bohrok used their powers to crumble mountains, level jungles and turn rivers to dust. Along with their smaller helpers, the **Bohrok Va**, the swarms were a menace beyond anything the Toa Nuva had ever known.

Tahnok
Pronunciation: TAH-nok

Colour: Red
Element: Fire

- Dangerous and unpredictable Bohrok, most often seen near Po-Koro and Ko-Koro
- Their fire shields can melt any substance on Mata Nui
- Built for swift and sudden movement, with lightning-fast reflexes

Tahnok Va
Pronunciation: TAH-nok VAH

Colour: Red
Element: Fire

- Skilled scouts who carry firestaffs for defence

Gahlok

Pronunciation: GAH-lok

Colour: Blue
Element: Water

- Masters of ambushing their foes, usually found near Ga-Koro or Onu-Koro
- Their water shields can draw water from any source and redirect it at a target
- Can blend in with the waves

Gahlok Va

Pronunciation: GAH-lok VAH

Colour: Blue
Element: Water

- Climb slippery rocks along the Mata Nui coastline with their sharp claws

Matoran Message:

Nuhvok

Pronunciation: NOO-vok

Colour: Black
Element: Earth

- Skilled tunnellers, active all over Mata Nui
- Can weaken Mata Nui structures from beneath, sending them tumbling down
- Have excellent night vision, but do not see well in bright sunlight

Nuhvok Va

Pronunciation: NOO-vok VAH

Colour: Black
Element: Earth

- Fast and fearless tunnellers

Lehvak
Pronunciation: LAY-vak

Colour: Green
Element: Swamp

- Can be found anywhere on the island but are best known for the damage they did to Le-Koro
- Secrete a powerful acid that can eat through any substance in seconds
- Operate in small groups, appearing and disappearing before they can be captured

Lehvak Va
Pronunciation: LAY-vak VAH

Colour: Green
Element: Swamp

- Equipped with small blades designed for cutting through dense jungle growth

Kohrak
Pronunciation: KOH-rak

Colour: Silver
Element: Ice

- The first Bohrok encountered by the Toa
- Use ice shields that can freeze anything, even molten rock or open flames
- Radiate such intense cold from their bodies that other Bohrok avoid them

Kohrak Va
Pronunciation: KOH-rak VAH

Colour: Silver
Element: Ice

- Can hide in a snowbank for days on end
- Climb icy slopes using their sharp claws

Krana

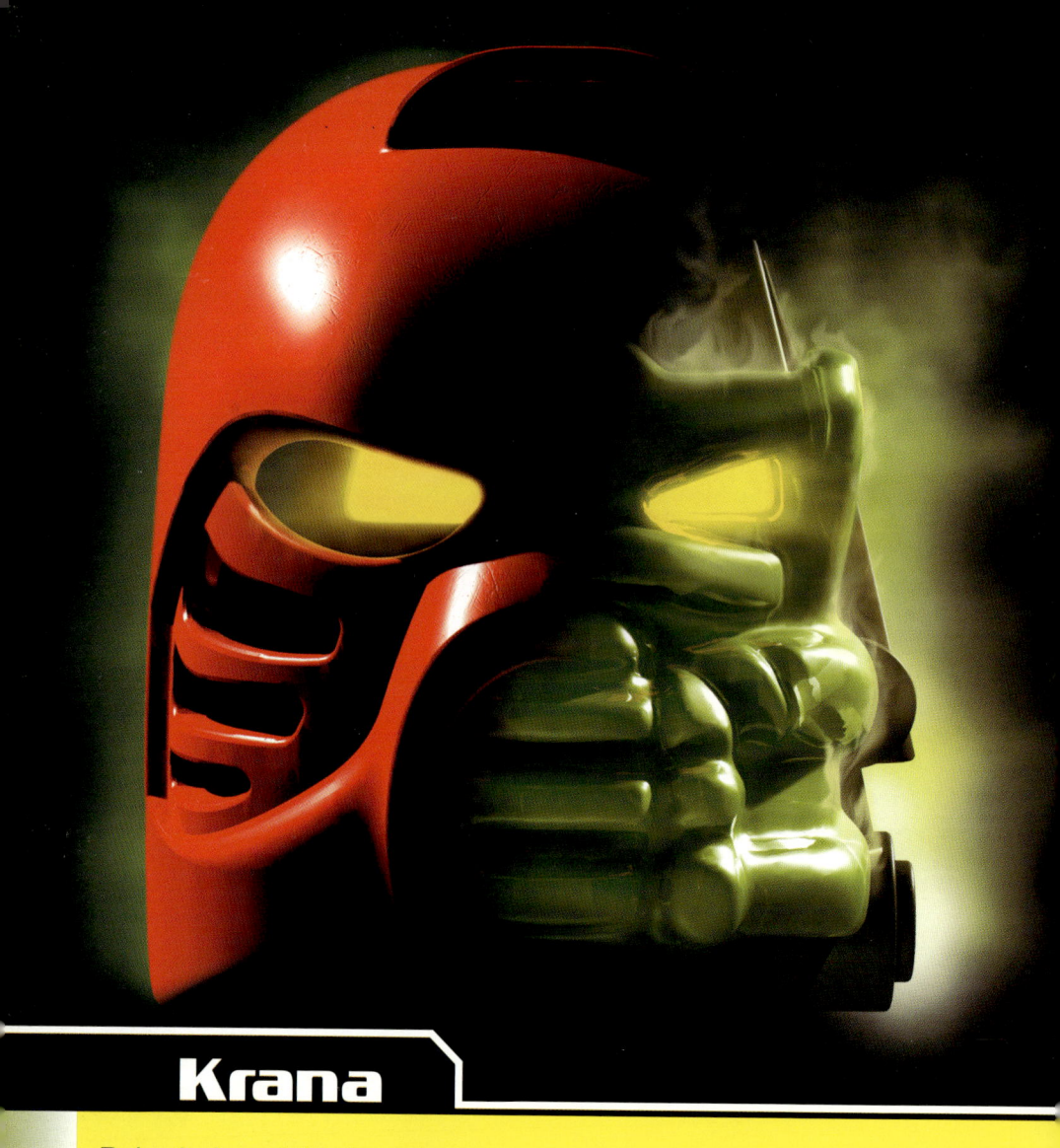

Bohrok do not think on their own. They are like empty vehicles that hold little brains called **krana**. The krana were linked to Cahdok and Gahdok, and received their orders from the swarm queens. When a krana was removed from a Bohrok, that Bohrok ceased to function properly and could be tamed.

There are a total of 48 krana (eight different types in the six colours of the different swarms). Each of the eight types of krana gives its Bohrok a different power or ability. Bohrok are especially dangerous because they can eject their krana on to the face of an opponent, which then takes control and links the opponent to the rest of the Bohrok swarm.

Krana Bo
Power: Infrared
- Gives its Bohrok the ability to see in the dark

Krana Ca
Power: Shielding
- Gives its Bohrok the power to shield itself and others from attack

Krana Ja
Power: Radar
- Can detect distant obstacles in the swarm's path

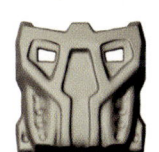

Krana Su
Power: Strength
- Has great energy and favours only the strongest Bohrok

Krana Vu
Power: Limited flight
- Gives its Bohrok the ability to fly short distances

Krana Xa
Power: Strategist
- Lives in the swarm commander, giving it the power to create complex plans

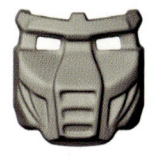

Krana Yo
Power: Tunnelling
- Gives its Bohrok the power to dig through any substance on the island

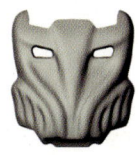

Krana Za
Power: Telepathy
- Has the ability to communicate telepathically with the other krana of the swarm

Pahrak
Pronunciation: PAH-rak

Colour: Brown
Element: Stone
- Have been seen all over the island of Mata Nui
- Shields give off seismic waves that can make mountains crumble to dust
- Slow-moving but powerful, they are almost impossible to stop

Pahrak Va
Pronunciation: PAH-rak VAH

Colour: Brown
Element: Stone
- Slow-moving Bohrok Va; the easiest to track down and capture

Cahdok and **Gahdok** were the queens of the Bohrok swarms. They possessed all the powers of the six Bohrok species, and they telepathically controlled all the krana. They were also symbiotic, which means they drew strength from each other. The closer Cahdok was to Gahdok, the more powerful they both became.

To defeat the Bohrok queens, the Toa were forced to combine their powers into one beam of energy. This energy beam created protodermis. Cahdok and Gahdok were trapped in the protodermis and could no longer command the krana, so the Bohrok swarms were no longer a threat to Mata Nui.

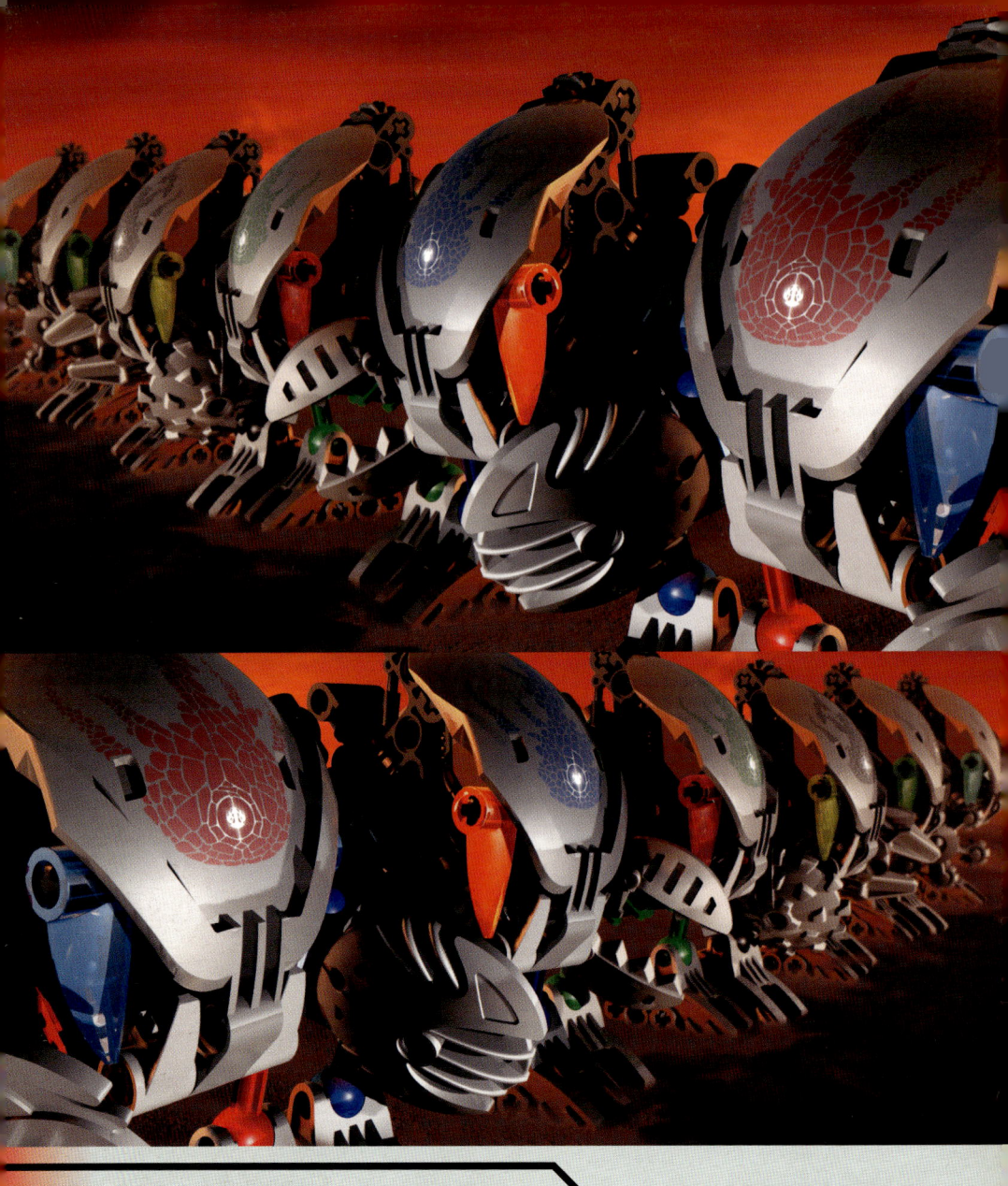

BOHROK-KAL

The six **Bohrok-Kal** were a special team of Bohrok with one mission: to free Cahdok and Gahdok from their imprisonment. Once free, the Bohrok queens would again unleash the Bohrok swarms. The Bohrok-Kal were given unique powers and were far more dangerous than ordinary Bohrok. It would take everything the Toa Nuva had to defeat these powerful foes.

Tahnok-Kal

Pronunciation: TAH-nok KAHL

Colour: Red
Power: Electricity
Shield: Electric shield; controls the forces of electricity; can hurl lightning bolts or create a defensive shield of electrical energy

Tahnok-Kal is the leader of the Bohrok-Kal squad. It was the first to discover that stealing the Toa Nuva symbols would rob the Toa Nuva of their powers.

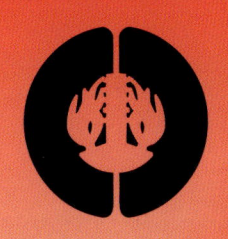

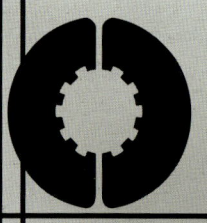

Nuhvok-Kal

Pronunciation: NOO-vok KAHL

Colour: Black
Power: Gravity
Shield: Gravity shield; can increase gravity and make its opponents superheavy or eliminate gravity, making opponents float away

Nuhvok-Kal is slow-moving but extremely powerful. Nuhvok-Kal was easily able to defeat Tahu Nuva by increasing gravity and sending Tahu plunging into the earth.

Bohrok-Kal Tools

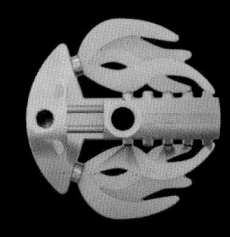

- Electric Shield: Capable of containing and releasing hundreds of thousands of watts of electricity at one time. Carried by Tahnok-Kal

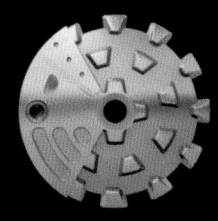

- Gravity Shield: Able to completely eliminate gravity in a large area or increase gravity by as much as 1,000 times normal. Carried by Nuhvok-Kal

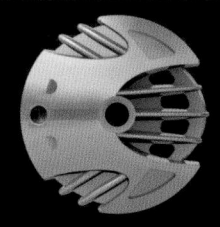

- Magnetic Shield: Able to create a magnetic force field so strong it could resist Tahu Nuva's full power. Carried by Gahlok-Kal

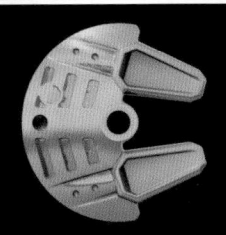

- Plasma Shield: Able to focus a stream of super-heated plasma at a temperature of roughly 2,000 degrees. Carried by Pahrak-Kal

- Sonic Shield: A sonic barrier created by this shield will respond to blows with a burst of sound so loud it can stun even a Toa Nuva. Carried by Kohrak-Kal

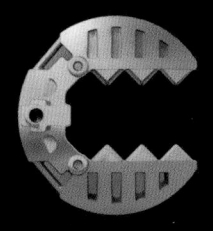

- Vacuum Shield: Can absorb and hold a huge amount of air for a long period of time before releasing it in a powerful blast. Carried by Lehvak-Kal

Krana-Kal

Like the Bohrok, each of the Bohrok-Kal carries within it a krana-kal. The krana-kal are living creatures capable of independent thought and communication with other species.

Krana Bo-Kal
Power: X-Ray Vision
- Can see in the dark and through most substances; only the walls of the caves and tunnels beneath Mata Nui can block this X-Ray Vision

Krana Ca-Kal
Power: Mind Link
- Linked to the minds of the Bohrok queens and can sense their presence

Krana Ja-Kal
Power: Radar Sense
- Can detect distant obstacles; magnifies the senses of its Bohrok-Kal, particularly hearing and smell

Krana Su-Kal
Power: Strength
- Gives its Bohrok-Kal tremendous strength and endurance; helps it resist heat and cold

Krana Vu-Kal
Power: Speed
- Can use a Bohrok-Kal to move across the ground or through the air at high speeds

Krana Xa-Kal
Power: Unlock
- The most important of the krana-kal; its touch will awaken the Bohrok queens

Krana Yo-Kal
Power: Sense Weakness
- Can sense stress points in the earth, allowing its Bohrok-Kal to tunnel through the ground more easily; can also sense underground movement

Krana Za-Kal
Power: Telepathy
- Can communicate telepathically with the other krana-kal; can also read other minds and sense strong emotion in the area

Gahlok-Kal

Pronunciation: GAH-lok KAHL

Colour: Blue
Power: Magnetism
Shield: Magnetic shield; can create a defence shield or can be used against an opponent

Gahlok-Kal is silent, stealthy and able to flow around any obstacles in its way. Its power was strong enough to pin Lewa Nuva to the ground.

Lehvak-Kal

Pronunciation: LAY-vak KAHL

Colour: Green
Power: Vacuum
Shield: Vacuum shield; can suck all the air out of a given area, or release it in a single blast that can shatter solid rock

Lehvak-Kal relies on ambush, clever tactics and surprise. It prefers to stay in Le-Wahi, where it can disappear into the jungle.

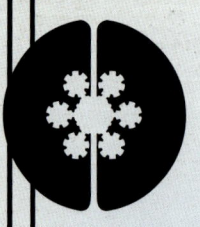

Kohrak-Kal

Pronunciation: KOH-rak KAHL

Colour: Silver
Power: Sonics
Shield: Sonic shield; can form a barrier of solid sound, make objects stress and shatter, or create solid objects made of sound

Kohrak-Kal is often seen on its own, because its powers are so great they can even affect other Bohrok-Kal. It is the easiest of the Bohrok-Kal to track, because the use of its powers creates sonic booms.

Pahrak-Kal
Pronunciation: PAH-rak KAHL

Colour: Brown
Power: Plasma
Shield: Plasma shield; can superheat any substance and turn it to molten liquid

Pahrak-Kal is slow, but it has plenty of power to make up for its lack of speed. It discovered the location of the Bohrok queens and led the rest of the squad to find them.

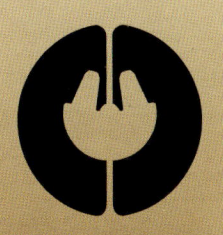

RAHKSHI

When the Mask of Light was discovered and the prophecy of the seventh Toa began to come true, Makuta unleashed the six Rahkshi. The Rahkshi are the ultimate hunters. They never tire, they never grow hungry and they never let any obstacle stand between them and their goal. With their Staffs of Power, they can overcome anything or anyone that stands in their way. Completely loyal to Makuta, they will do whatever he commands. And now he has commanded them to seek out the Herald of the Seventh Toa, who is on a journey to find the Toa of Light. When the Rahkshi have found this Herald, the Rahkshi will bring him or her to Makuta.

The Toa Nuva *must* stop the Rahkshi from finding the Herald. Otherwise, the seventh Toa may never be found.

Panrahk

Pronunciation: PAN-rahk

Colour: Brown

Type: Fragmenter

Staff of Power: Makes any object fly into tiny fragments

Panrahk is the most 'explosive' of the Rahkshi, with lightning-fast reflexes. The only warning of his approach is that the ground beneath his feet blows up in a series of tiny explosions when he walks.

Guurahk

Pronunciation: GER-rahk

Colour: Blue

Type: Disintegrator

Staff of Power: Releases a cone-shaped energy wave that makes an object crumble to dust

Guurahk will spend hours observing an enemy before striking. He analyzes every strength and weakness of his foe before he acts.

Lerahk

Pronunciation: LAY-rahk

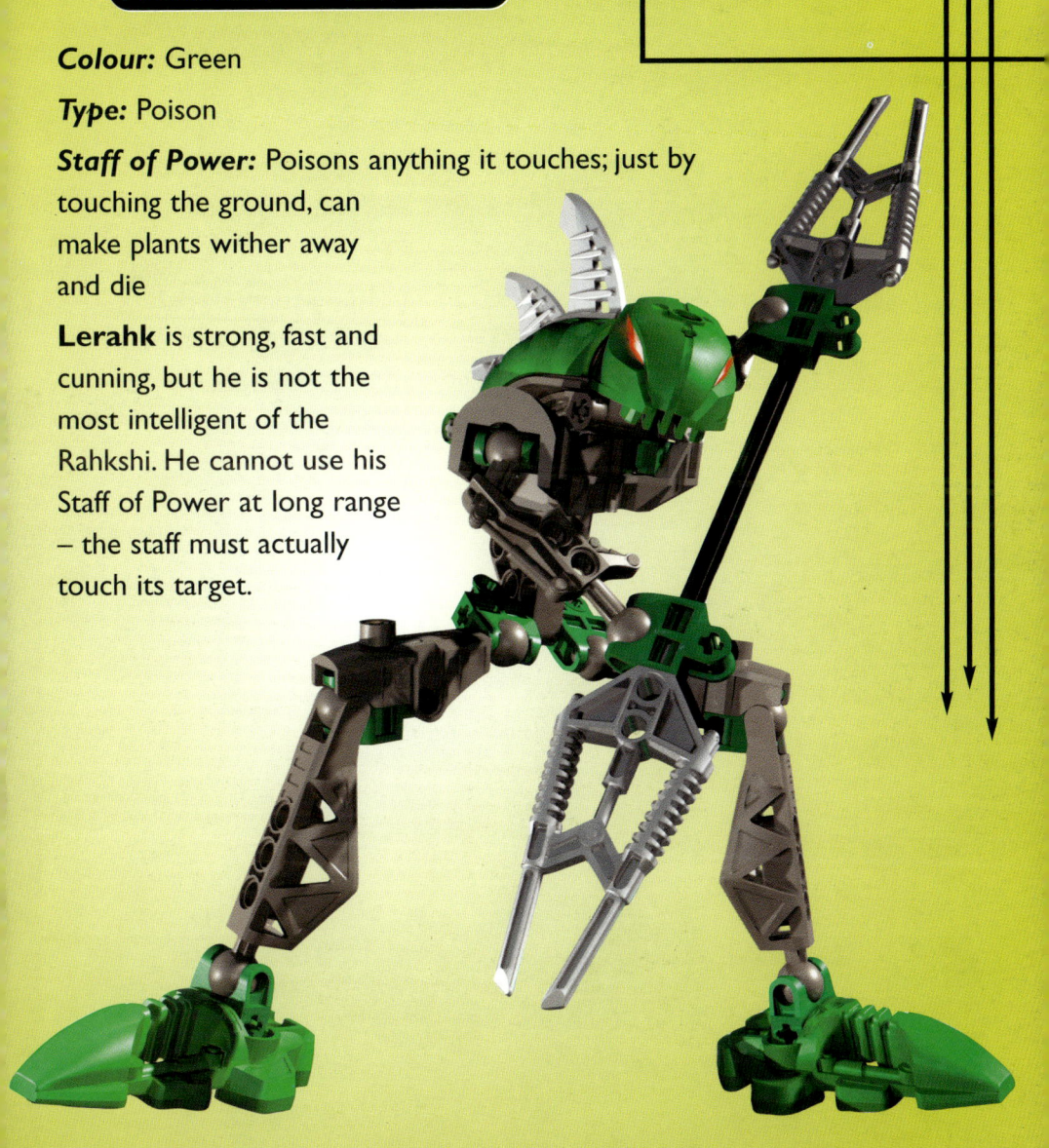

Colour: Green

Type: Poison

Staff of Power: Poisons anything it touches; just by touching the ground, can make plants wither away and die

Lerahk is strong, fast and cunning, but he is not the most intelligent of the Rahkshi. He cannot use his Staff of Power at long range – the staff must actually touch its target.

Matoran Message:

Kurahk

Pronunciation: KER-rahk

Colour: White
Type: Anger
Staff of Power: Sends anger energy at an opponent, making the target angry with everyone around him, even friends

Kurahk is always in a rage and often acts recklessly. It is possible that his anger actually increases his powers. Makuta hoped that Kurahk would destroy the unity of the Toa Nuva by turning them against one another.

Turahk

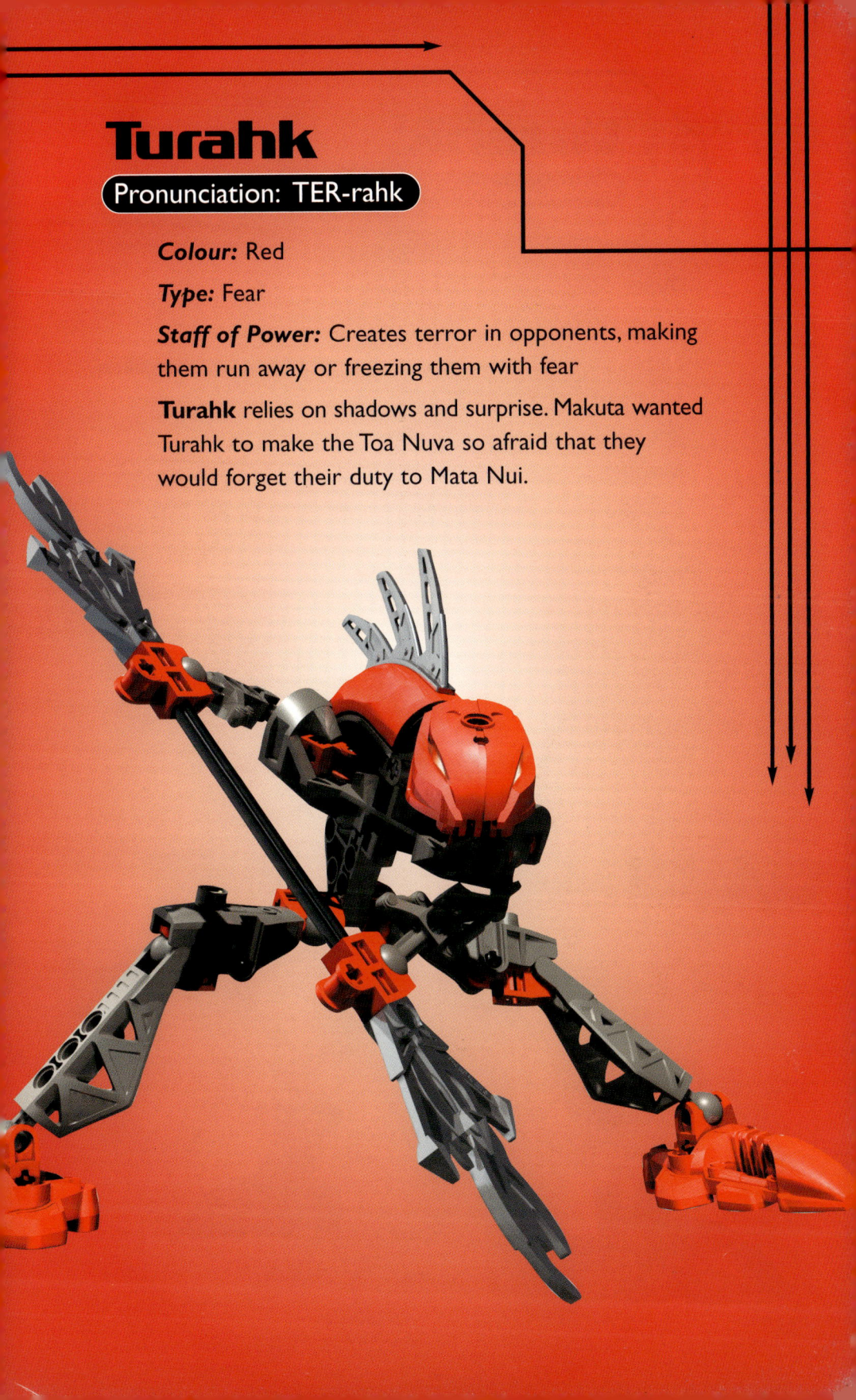

Pronunciation: TER-rahk

Colour: Red

Type: Fear

Staff of Power: Creates terror in opponents, making them run away or freezing them with fear

Turahk relies on shadows and surprise. Makuta wanted Turahk to make the Toa Nuva so afraid that they would forget their duty to Mata Nui.

Vorahk

Pronunciation: VOH-rahk

Colour: Black

Type: Weakener

Staff of Power: Can drain the energy of a foe, which allows Vorahk to absorb it; as his opponents grow weaker, he grows stronger; his staff must be in physical contact with its target

Vorahk is the best hunter of all the Rahkshi. His opponents have no hope of hiding from him. Makuta hoped that Vorahk would sap the Toa Nuva's strength, making it impossible for them to achieve their destiny.

Kraata

Within each Rahkshi is a leech-like creature called a **kraata**. The kraata gives the Rahkshi the power and intelligence needed to carry out its mission.

But kraata first appeared on the island of Mata Nui a long time before the Rahkshi came into being – they are a part of Makuta. They move like snakes across the ground, and wherever they go, they spread infection. Makuta used the kraata to take over the island's Rahi.

The Turaga have done their best to track down and trap kraata all over the island. These kraata are then sealed away in special containers, and the containers are hidden in a vast cave. If these kraata were ever unleashed, a shadow plague would strike Mata Nui. All of the Matoran might become infected by Makuta's darkness.

The Saga Continues . . .

This is just the beginning of the exciting BIONICLE™ story – many new challenges lie ahead for the Toa Nuva.

But they are ready – they are pledged to defeat
Makuta and rescue Mata Nui, *whatever it takes!*